Preschool Art
Clay and Dough

MaryAnn F. Kohl
Illustrations: Katheryn Davis

Dedication

Dedicated in memory of my grandmother, Mary Geanne Faubion Wilson,
the first published author I ever knew, who sparked my imagination
when she told me that angels made my freckles
when they kissed me on the nose as I slept.

Acknowledgments

I would like to thank my editor, Kathy Charner, for her humor and kindness
in our editor-author relationship. Sometimes I think we have too much fun to call this work!
In addition, I would like to thank the owners of Gryphon House, Leah and Larry Rood,
for their support and friendship, and their belief in this book and in me.
Most important, my thanks go to my husband, Michael,
and my daughters, Hannah and Megan, who keep my mind clear,
tell me when I've been wonderful or when I haven't, and
remind me of what is most important in life.

Preschool Art

Clay
and
Dough

It's the process, not the product!

MaryAnn F. Kohl

gryphon house®, inc.
Beltsville, Maryland

Library of Congress Cataloging-in-Publication Data

Kohl, MaryAnn F.,
    Preschool art: it's the process, not the product! / MaryAnn F. Kohl; [illustrations, Katheryn Davis].
        p.   cm.
    "A MaryAnn Kohl book."
    Inludes indexes.
    Contents: [1] Craft and construction --[2] Clay, dough, and sculpture -- [3] collage and paper -- [4] Painting -- [5] Drawing.
    ISBN 0-87659-250-7 (v.2)
    1. Art--Study and teaching (Preschool)--Handbooks, manuals, etc. I. Title: craft and construction. II. Title: Clay, dough, and sculpture. III. Title: Collage and paper. IV. Title: Painting. V. Title: Drawing. VI. Davis, Katheryn. VII. Title.
LB1140.5.A7 K64 2001
372.5'044--dc21
                                                                                    2001018468

Illustrations: Katheryn Davis
Cover photograph: Straight Shots Product Photography, Ellicott City, Maryland.

Bulk purchase

Gryphon House books are available at special discount when purchased in bulk for special premiums and sales promotions as well as for fund-raising use. Special editions or book excerpts also can be created to specification. For details, contact the Director of Marketing at the address above.

Disclaimer

The publisher and the author cannot be held responsible for injury, mishap, or damages incurred during the use of or because of the activities in this book. The author recommends appropriate and reasonable supervision at all times based on the age and capability of each child.

Table of Contents

It's the Process, Not the Product

Why is art process important?

Young children do art for the experience, the exploration, and the experimentation. In the "process" of doing art, they discover creativity, mystery, joy, and frustration, which are all important pieces in the puzzle of learning. Whatever the resulting masterpiece—be it a bright, sticky glob or a gallery-worthy piece—it is only a result to the young child, not the reason for doing the art in the first place.

Art process allows children to explore, discover, and manipulate their worlds. Sometimes the process is sensory, such as feeling slippery cool paint on bare fingers. Other times it is the mystery of colors blending unexpectedly, or the surprise of seeing a realistic picture evolve from a random blob of paint. Art process can be a way to "get the wiggles out," or to smash a ball of clay instead of another child.

How can adults encourage the process of art?

Provide interesting materials. Stand back and watch. Offer help with unruly materials, but keep hands off children's work as much as possible. It's a good idea not to make samples for children to copy because this limits their possibilities.

Sometimes adults unknowingly communicate to a child that the product is the most important aspect of the child's art experience. The following comments and questions serve as examples of things to say that will help encourage each child to evaluate his or her own artwork:

Tell me about your artwork.

What part did you like the best?

I see you've used many colors!

Did you enjoy making this?

How did the paint feel?

The yellow is so bright next to the purple!

How did you make such a big design?

I see you made your own brown color. How did you do it?

Process art is a wonder to behold. Watch the children discover their unique capabilities and the joy of creating. This is where they begin to feel good about art and to believe that mistakes can be a stepping stone instead of a roadblock—in art as well as in other aspects of their lives. A concept children enjoy hearing is, "There's no right way, there's no wrong way, there's just your way."

Getting Ready!

Being prepared makes art experiences all the more enjoyable.
Here are some tips for success:

Covered Workspace

Cover the workspace—whether it is a table, floor, chair, wall, or countertop—with newspaper. Tape it down to prevent wiggles and spills of art materials. It's so much easier to bunch up sheets of paint-filled, sticky newspaper and find a clean space underneath than to clean up uncovered workspaces time and again. Other workspace coverings that work well are sheets of cardboard, an old shower curtain, a plastic tablecloth, big butcher paper, and roll ends of newsprint from the local newspaper print shop.

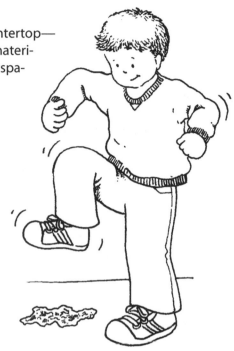

Handy Cleanup

Make cleanup easy and independent for young artists. All the less worry for the adult in charge! Place a wet sponge or pads of damp paper towels next to the art project for a simple way to wipe fingers as needed. Rather than have children running to the sink, fill a bucket with warm soapy water and place it next to the work area. Then add a few old towels for drying hands. Damp rags and sponges are handy for wiping spills, tidying up, and cleaning splatters as needed.

The Cover-up

An old apron, Dad's old shirt (sleeves cut off), a smock, and a paint shirt are all helpful cover-ups for creative preschoolers. Instead, consider this: wear old play clothes and old shoes and call them "art clothes," used for art only. It's a wonderful feeling to get into art without being concerned about protecting clothing. These clothes become more unique with time and are often a source of pride!

Other Tips

- Create a separate drying area covered with newspapers. Allow wet projects to dry completely.
- Always protect a larger circle of space than the immediate area around the project. Think about floors, walls, and carpets (maybe even ceilings!).
- Shallow containers are often mentioned in the Materials lists. These include cookie sheets, flat baking pans, clean kitty litter trays, plastic cafeteria trays, painter's pans, and flat dishes and plates.
- It's never too late to start collecting recyclables for art. Save collage materials, fabric and paper scraps, Styrofoam grocery trays, yarn, sewing trims, and even junk mail.
- Wash hands thoroughly before starting any edible activity.
- Do activities inside or out unless specifically noted as an outdoor activity only.

Using the Icons

Each page has icons that help make the projects in Clay and Dough more useable and accessible. The icons are suggestions only. Experiment with the materials, vary the suggested techniques, and modify the projects to suit the needs and abilities of each child.

Age
The age icon indicates the general age range of when a child can create and explore independently without much adult assistance. The "& Up" means that older children will enjoy the project, and that younger children might need more assistance. Children do not always fit the standard developmental expectations of a particular age, so decide which projects suit individual children and their abilities and needs.

Planning and Preparation
The plan and prep icon indicates the degree of planning or preparation time an adult will need to collect materials, set up the activity, and supervise the activity. Icons shown indicate planning that is easy or short, medium or moderate, or long and more involved.

Help
The help icon indicates the child may need extra assistance with certain steps during the activity from an adult or even from another child.

Caution
The caution icon appears for activities requiring materials that may be sharp, hot, or electrical in nature. These activities require extra supervision and care.

Edible
Indicates activities that are safe to eat.

Hints
Hints are suggestions for the adults working with the artists.

Great Goop

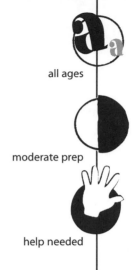

all ages

moderate prep

help needed

Materials
cornstarch
water
large measuring cup
spoon
food coloring, optional
plastic tub or large baking pan

Art Process

1. Mix equal parts of cornstarch and water in a large measuring cup.
   For example, mix 1 cup (125 g) cornstarch with 1 cup (240 ml) water. Make as much as desired.
2. Add food coloring, if desired.
3. Pour the mixture into a plastic tub or large baking pan.
4. Experience and enjoy this mixture's unique properties and surprises.

Variations

· Experiment by adding more cornstarch or more water to the mixture.
· For a group experience, make Great Goop in a water table or large tub. Use utensils such as spatulas, rolling pins, or whisks to manipulate the mixture.

MIX CORNSTARCH
WITH WATER...

Hints

· To discard the mixture, scoop it into a paper or plastic bag and place it in the trash. Do not pour it down the drain.
· This is a very messy but wonderful project!

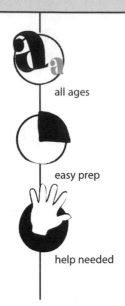

all ages

easy prep

help needed

Gak
(Homemade Silly Putty)

Materials
food coloring
measuring cup
white glue
plastic container
liquid starch

Art Process
1. Add food coloring to 1 cup (240 ml) of glue in a plastic container.
2. Stir in 1 cup (240 ml) liquid starch, adding a little at a time. Stir the mixture until it holds together like putty. (Test it with your fingers: if it is too sticky, add more starch in small amounts until it is smooth and rubbery.)
3. Have fun pulling, stretching, and bouncing it.
4. Store the Gak in a plastic bag or an airtight container.

Variation
• Stretch the Gak over a Sunday comic strip and press down. Then, place the Gak on a piece of paper to "transfer" the drawing.

Hint
• Elmer's glue works well for this project.

Paint Dough

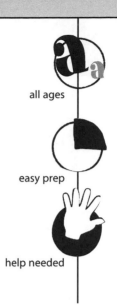

all ages

easy prep

help needed

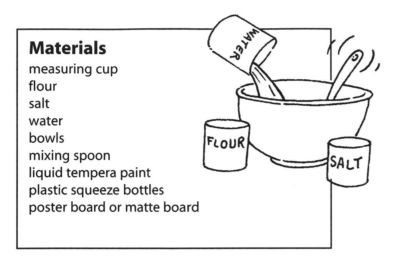

Materials
measuring cup
flour
salt
water
bowls
mixing spoon
liquid tempera paint
plastic squeeze bottles
poster board or matte board

Art Process
1. Mix equal parts of flour, salt, and water in a bowl and stir it until it has a paste-like consistency.
2. Add liquid tempera paint to the mixture. Make several different colors in separate bowls.
3. Pour each colored paint mixture into a plastic squeeze bottle.
4. Squeeze paint onto a poster board or matte board and make designs.

Hints
- The salt will add a glistening, crystal-like quality to the design.
- When different colors or paint mixtures bump into each other, they will not mix together. Instead, they will maintain their own separate design and space, which is interesting to explore.
  - The paint mixture may dry and harden in squeeze bottles, so rinse out the bottles when artists finish the project.

all ages

moderate prep

help needed

Squishy Mixture

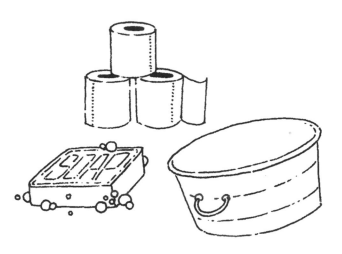

Materials
3 rolls of toilet paper
large tub
warm water
old cheese grater
bar of soap,
   preferably Ivory
Soap
Borax
food coloring,
   optional

Art Process
1. Unroll three rolls of toilet paper into a large tub.
2. Tear the toilet paper into pieces.
3. Add enough warm water to saturate the paper.
4. Grate one bar of soap and add it to the toilet paper mixture.
5. Add ⅓ cup (80 ml) Borax.
6. Mix it together using your hands, squishing and squashing it to enjoy the way it feels. (This mixture is not great for molding; it simply serves as a wonderful sensory experience.)
7. If desired, mix in food coloring.

Variations
- Press the Squishy Dough into measuring cups and small molds, squish it into a garlic press, or use it with sand toys.
- Bury objects in the Squishy Mixture. Then, shovel and rake through it to find them. Play pirates or paleontologists!
- Add tempera paint or liquid watercolor to the Squishy Dough. Try mixing colors to make new colors.
- Bury large marbles and/or the smaller "porcupine balls" (Koosh balls). Sit around the tub and use your feet to find the marbles and balls!

Hint
- Squishy Mixture will keep for several days if you place it in an airtight container or cover the tub with foil or plastic wrap.

No-Cook Playdough

all ages

moderate prep

help needed

Materials

measuring cups and
  spoons
cold water
salt
oil
bowl
mixing spoon
powdered paint,
  optional
flour
cornstarch
cutting board

Art Process

1. Mix 1 cup (240 ml) cold water, 1 cup (250 g)
    salt, and 2 teaspoons (10 ml) oil in a bowl.
2. If desired, add powdered paint to the mixture.
3. Gradually stir in 3 cups (375 g) flour and 2
    tablespoons (20 g) cornstarch and mix
    it to a bread-dough consistency.
4. Pour the dough onto a cutting board and knead with your hands.
5. Use this dough like modeling clay.

2 tsp. Oil

Variation

• Color the dough using food coloring or paste coloring.

Hint

• This quick and easy clay does not
  dry well, but it is pliable, bright,
  and colorful.

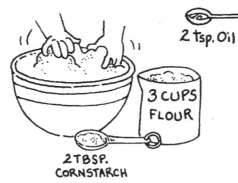

2 TBSP.
CORNSTARCH

3 CUPS
FLOUR

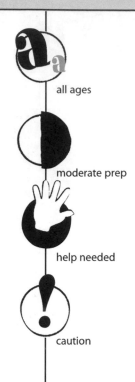

all ages

moderate prep

help needed

caution

Cooked Playdough

Materials
measuring cups and
  spoons
flour
water
salt
cream of tartar
pan
food coloring,
  optional
stove
spoon
cutting board
cooking utensils and
  tools
plastic container
  with lid

Art Process

1. Mix 1 cup (125 g) flour, 1 cup (240 ml) water, 1 cup (250 g) salt, and 1 tablespoon (15 ml) cream of tartar in a pan. (To make colored dough, add food coloring to the cup of water before mixing it with the other ingredients.)
2. Place the pan on the stove over low heat (supervise closely). Stir the dough to form a ball.
3. Remove the pan from the stove.
4. Pour the ball onto a cutting board and knead until it is smooth and pliable.
5. Begin sculpting, exploring, playing, and creating with the warm dough. Explore using a variety of utensils and tools, such as a rolling pin or wooden dowel, cookie cutter, nuts and bolts, or a garlic press.
6. The dough will last for a week or so if stored in a covered plastic container.

STIR UNTIL DOUGH
FORMS A BALL...

Hints

• When the playdough begins to crack and crumble, it's time to make a fresh batch.
• Double this recipe and experience twice the fun!

Tutti Fruitti Playdough

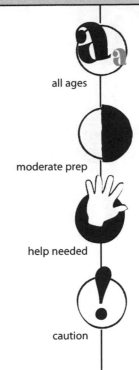

all ages

moderate prep

help needed

caution

Materials

medium saucepan
stove
measuring cups and
   spoons
flour
salt
cream of tartar
unsweetened
   powdered fruit
   drink such as
   Kool-Aid
mixing spoon
water
vegetable oil
plastic bag

Art Process

1. Place a medium saucepan on top of the stove.
2. Mix 1 cup (125 g) flour, ¼ cup (60 g) salt, 2 table-spoons (30 g) cream of tartar, and 1 package of unsweetened powdered fruit drink in the saucepan.
3. Add 1 cup (240 ml) water and 1 tablespoon (15 ml) oil to the mixture.
4. Turn on the stove and stir the mixture over medium heat for 3 to 5 minutes (supervise closely).
5. Remove the mixture from the stove when it forms a ball.
6. Using your hands, knead the ball until it is smooth.
7. Play and explore with this fragrant, brightly colored dough.
8. To store the mixture, put in a plastic bag and refrigerate it.

2 TBSP CREAM OF TARTAR

1 CUP FLOUR

1 CUP WATER

1 TBSP. OIL

THEN ADD...

KOOL AID

¼ CUP SALT

MIX THESE TOGETHER

STIR OVER MEDIUM HEAT 3 TO 5 MINUTES.

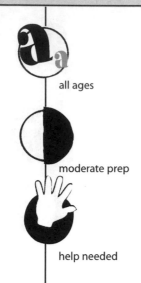

all ages

moderate prep

help needed

Soapy Clay

Art Process

1. Pour 2 cups (400 g) detergent flakes into a bowl.
2. Gradually add 2 tablespoons (30 ml) water, mixing and squeezing it with your hands to form a ball.
3. If desired, use colored water instead of clear water. Simply add food coloring to the water before adding it to the detergent flakes.
4. Add more water, if necessary.
5. Model and explore using the Soapy Clay. Squeeze it to form different shapes.

Materials
measuring cups and spoons
white detergent flakes, such as Ivory Snow
bowl
water
food coloring, optional

Variations

- Make soap balls or shapes to use at home or school, or give them as gifts.
- Mix natural materials into Soapy Clay, such as oatmeal or crushed dried flower petals.
- Add fragrance to the Soapy Clay using spices such as cinnamon or extracts such as almond or lemon.
- Try carving the Soapy Clay with a spoon, toothpick, or other tool. Supervise closely.

Hint

- An artist may accidentally put a soapy finger into his or her mouth. If this happens, help the artist rinse out his or her mouth with water until the taste is gone. If soap gets into someone's eye, flood the eye with clear water.

GRADUALLY ADD 2 TBSP. COLORED WATER ...

Playful Clay

Materials
measuring cups
baking soda
cornstarch
pan
mixing spoon
warm water
stove or hot plate
cutting board
food coloring or
　tempera paints
clear nail polish,
　optional

MIX TOGETHER

Art Process
1. Mix 1 cup (180 g) baking soda and ½ cup (60 g) cornstarch in a pan.
2. Add ⅔ cup (160 ml) warm water to the mixture and stir until smooth.
3. Place the pan over medium heat on the stove or hot plate. Stir the mixture as you bring it to a boil (supervise closely).
4. When the mixture reaches the consistency of mashed potatoes, pour it onto a cutting board to cool.
5. After the dough has cooled, knead it with your hands.
6. Knead food coloring into the clay. (You may also paint dry objects.)
7. Explore and create using the Playful Clay.
8. Allow creations to harden or dry for several hours.
9. If desired, paint the dry objects with clear nail polish to make them shiny.

BOIL & STIR

Variation
• Crush colored chalk and knead it into the dough to create a speckled coloring.

Hints
• This recipe yields 1½ cups of dough.
• Store the dough in an airtight container. It will keep for several weeks if it is not exposed to air.
• Dough hardens quickly.

POUR ONTO CUTTING BOARD

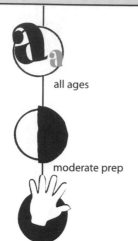

all ages

moderate prep

help needed

caution

Craft Clay

Art Process

1. Combine 4 cups (500 g) flour and 1 cup (250 g) salt in a bowl.
2. Create a hole in the center of the dry ingredients and pour in 1 cup (240 ml) warm water.
3. Mix the dough using your hands, adding more water as needed. Mix the dough until it forms a ball and is not crumbly or sticky.
4. Sprinkle flour onto a cutting board.
5. Place the dough on the floured cutting board and knead until smooth (about 5 minutes).
6. Place a small portion of dough on a piece of foil or wax paper.
7. Dip a brush or your fingers into water and mold the dough together to make sculptures.
8. Cover a baking sheet with aluminum foil and place completed sculptures or objects on it.
9. Turn the oven to 325° F, place the baking sheet into it, and bake the objects for 1 hour, or until they are hard. Tap objects with a knife—if the dough does not "give," the sculptures are done.
10. Wrap the rest of the dough in plastic and store in the refrigerator. (If it dries out, add a few drops of water and knead.)

Materials

measuring cups
flour
salt
bowl
mixing spoon
warm water
cutting board
foil or wax paper
plastic wrap
paintbrush, optional
aluminum foil
baking sheet
oven
knife

Variation

- Use Craft Clay to make napkin rings; picture frames; jewelry; beads; artificial rolls, bread, bagels, fruits, and vegetables; bugs and insects; animals; or holiday decorations.

BAKE AT 325° TIL HARD.

Hints

- Create sculptures directly on the baking sheet to prevent tearing when moving them.
- Repair breaks and cracks in baked objects by forcing white glue into the cracks. Or, press fresh dough between broken pieces, re-bake, and paint.

Yeast Dough

all ages

moderate prep

help needed

caution

edible!

Materials

measuring cups and
    spoons
warm water
large bowl
yeast
mixing spoon
salt
sugar
flour
cookie sheet
clean towel
grease
1 egg
cup
pastry brush
oven

STIR TIL SOFT   MIX TIL DOUGH FORMS
A BALL...

Art Process

1. Pour 1½ cups (360 ml) warm water into a large bowl.
2. Sprinkle 1 package of yeast into the water and stir until it is soft.
3. Add 1 teaspoon (7 g) salt, 1 tablespoon (20 g) sugar, and 4 cups (500 g) flour. Mix the ingredients together to form a ball.
4. Sprinkle flour onto the work surface and place the dough on it.
5. Knead the dough until it is smooth and elastic.
6. Roll and twist the dough into shapes, such as letters or animals.
7. Rub a light layer of grease over the cookie sheet. Place the dough sculptures on the cookie sheet and cover it with a clean towel. Place it in a warm area to let the dough rise.
8. Beat an egg. After the dough sculptures have doubled in size, brush each one with the beaten egg. If desired, sprinkle salt on them.
9. Turn the oven to 350° F, place the dough sculptures in the oven, and bake for 12 to 15 minutes, until they are firm and golden brown.
10. Remove the baking sheet from the oven. Let them cool slightly, eat, and enjoy! Yum!

1½ CUPS WARM WATER

Variation

•   Use this delicious dough to make a healthy alternative to seasonal treats such as jack-o-lanterns in the fall, snowflakes in the winter, bunnies in the spring, and great big suns in the summer.

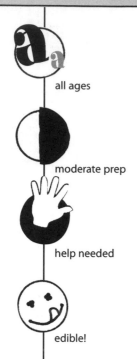

all ages

moderate prep

help needed

edible!

Peanut Butter Dough

NON-FAT DRY MILK

Materials

measuring cups and
  spoons
peanut butter
non-fat powdered
  milk
bowl
honey, optional

Art Process

1. Add equal parts of peanut butter and dry milk in a bowl. Mix them together using your hands.
2. Add honey, if desired.
3. Knead and mix the dough until it is stiff.
4. Model and experiment with the peanut butter dough (use it like play-dough).
5. Eat and enjoy your creation!

Variation

- Add other ingredients to the dough, such as raisins, shredded coconut, chocolate chips, or bits of dry breakfast cereal, or use these ingredients to decorate the designs.

Hints

- One cup of peanut butter and 1 cup of dry milk makes a nice amount of dough for one child.
- Artists can easily model with this dough, but it does not harden.
- Store leftover dough in a covered container in the refrigerator.

MIX EQUAL PARTS IN A BOWL!

DRY MILK

PEANUT BUTTER

Brick Making

moderate prep

help needed

caution

Materials

dirt
plastic bucket
water
muffin tins or ice
cube trays
warm area or oven
newsprint

PAT THEM FLAT ON TOP!

Art Process

1. Put dirt in a plastic bucket and mix in just enough water to form a mud ball.
2. Press the mud into muffin tin cups or ice cube tray sections.
3. Place the tins or trays in a warm place for about 10 days, or bake at 250° F for 15 minutes.
4. Place a piece of newsprint on the floor.
5. After the mud has dried or cooled, drop the "bricks" onto the newsprint and see which ones break and which ones hold together.
6. Use the solid bricks to make buildings.

Hints

- Make as many bricks as possible to make building more fun.
- Add some plaster of Paris to the mud mixture to help it hold together better.
- Experiment using different amounts of plaster of Paris.
- Review the building suggestions for Brick Building (page 22).

involved prep

Brick Building

Materials

homemade dirt bricks
   (see Brick Making, page 21)
plaster of Paris or dirt
water
building items (see list)

Art Process

1. Make homemade
   dirt bricks (see page 21).
2. Mix water and plaster of Paris to a runny
   consistency, or mix water with dirt to make mud.
3. Attach bricks and other building items (see list) to make a free-form
   building. Use the plaster of Paris or mud as "cement" to hold it all together.
4. Dip, paint, or spoon plaster over various building items and add them to the
   building.
5. Allow the project to dry overnight or longer.

Variations

- Use wood scraps and glue to make buildings.
- Build edible structures using sugar cubes and Royal Icing art (page 50).

Building Items

rocks, stones, or gravel
sticks
weeds

Hint

- Some children do not like to get their hands dirty; sometimes this is merely
  a stage. Be understanding—this project is not for everyone.

A PYRAMID!

Earth Clay Explore

Materials
tape
heavy garbage bag
earth clay, sometimes called
  moist clay
tools (see list)

Art Process
1. Tape a heavy garbage bag to a table to protect the work area.
2. Place earth clay on the garbage bag.
3. Roll, squeeze, pound, press, and form earth clay in any manner desired using various tools (see list).
4. Allow the clay objects to dry. Or, place the clay in an airtight container and reuse it later.

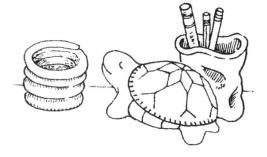

Hints
- Purchase earth clay at craft shops, art supply stores, and school supply stores.
- Clay can clog drains, so do not wash it down the sink. Instead, wash hands and utensils in a bucket or tub of water and discard the water outside.
- This activity is messy, but it is very rewarding and artistically satisfying.

Tools
blocks
butter knives
cookie cutters
garlic press
rolling pin
spatula
toothpicks
toy pieces

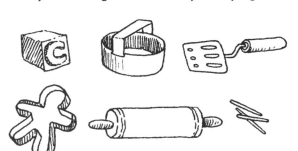

age 3 & up

involved prep

help needed

Earth Clay Sculpture

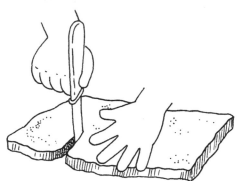

Materials
tape
heavy garbage bag
earth clay,
   sometimes called
   moist clay
rolling pin or
   cylinder block
blunt knife
tools, such as a
   spatula, cookie
   cutter, or garlic
   press
tempera paints
paintbrushes
clear gloss enamel
   or lacquer,
   optional

Art Process

1. Tape a heavy garbage bag to a table to protect the work area.
2. Place a small portion of earth clay on the garbage bag.
3. Using a rolling pin, roll out the clay to a thickness of about ½" (1 cm).
4. Cut out a shape, such as a fish, square, heart, or leaf, using a blunt knife (such as a butter knife).
5. Press or cut designs into the clay using tools such as a spatula or cookie cutter.
6. Allow the clay shape to dry.
7. Paint designs onto the clay shapes.
8. Allow the paint to dry. Brush clear gloss enamel or lacquer over the sculpture, if desired.

Hint
• Store clay in an airtight container.

A KITCHEN TOOL HANDLE PRESSED AT AN ANGLE LOOKS LIKE SCALES OR FEATHERS!

IMPRESS A BUTTON IN THE CLAY FOR EYES!

Playdough Car and Track

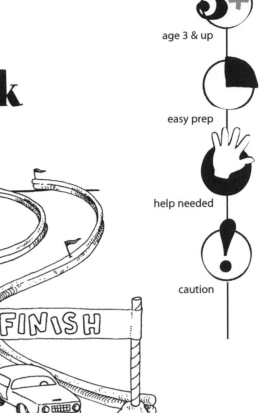

3+

age 3 & up

easy prep

help needed

caution

Materials

playdough (see recipe below or use any homemade recipe, or commercial play clay)
table
toy cars

Art Process

1. Roll playdough into long, thin sausage or snake shapes.
2. Arrange the snake shapes on the table. Connect them together to make walls.
3. Create matching walls about 3" (8 cm) from the first wall. The racing track will be between these walls.
4. Drive toy cars or roll playdough balls through the tracks. Have imaginative, pretend races and lots of fun.

Variations

- Draw lines on a piece of butcher paper. Cover the lines with rolls of playdough snakes and drive the cars between them.
- Build the tracks on a larger sheet of plywood or a board. Place the playdough board on an incline and roll the cars through the tracks.

Simple and Good Playdough

(requires stove-top cooking)

Materials

measuring cups and spoons
flour
water
salt
cream of tartar
oil
saucepan
food coloring, optional
stovetop or hot plate
wooden spoon
bread board

Mix 1 cup (125 g) flour, 1 cup (240 ml) water, ½ cup (125 g) salt, 2 teaspoons (10 g) cream of tartar, and 2 tablespoons (30 ml) oil in a saucepan. Add food coloring, if desired. Cook over low heat, stirring with a wooden spoon until it is thickened. Place dough on a bread board. Allow it to cool slightly and then knead. Double or triple this recipe as necessary. Store playdough in a covered container to keep it moist and pliable.

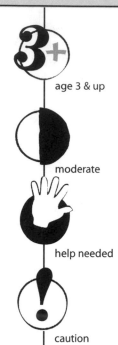

moderate

help needed

caution

Candle Holder

Art Process

1. Make homemade playdough (see pages 13-14).
2. Place a ball of play-dough into the aluminum pie plate and press it down to fill the plate.
3. Push a candle into the center of the playdough. (The fat pillar candle varieties work well for this project.)
4. Press other items into the playdough, such as pinecones, weeds, sticks, seed pods, and nuts.
5. To make a silver or gold candleholder, remove the candle and spray the play-dough with silver or gold paint.
6. If desired, sprinkle glitter onto the wet paint to add extra sparkle.
7. Allow the base to dry and then replace the candle.
8. Tie ribbons or bows to bobby pins and push them into the playdough.
9. Briefly light the candle and then snuff it out.

Materials

homemade playdough (see pages 13-14)
aluminum pie plate
candle
small pinecones, weeds, sticks, seed pods, and nuts
silver or gold spray paint, optional
glitter, optional
ribbons
bobby pins

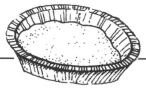

Hints

- Never let candles burn unattended because the materials in this project are flammable.
- This project requires one-on-one adult supervision the entire time the candle is lit.
- A safer variation (although one that still requires supervision) is to set a votive candle inside a small, clear jar and place it in the playdough candle holder. The glass jar will help contain the flame.

Nature Garden

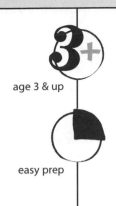

age 3 & up

easy prep

Materials

playdough
heavy paper plate
seeds and weeds (see list)

Art Process

1. Place a ball of playdough in the center of a heavy paper plate.
2. Spread the playdough out to the sides of the plate. Add more playdough, if necessary, to completely cover the plate.
3. Poke leaves, flowers, and other objects from outdoors into the playdough to make a "garden."
4. If desired, press some of the leaves or weeds flat into the playdough.
5. Place the finished Nature Garden in the center of a table or on a shelf.

Variations

- Make a miniature garden in an egg carton cup or on a small paper plate.
- Place small figures or toys in the garden.
- Add a small mirror to the garden and partially bury it with playdough to simulate a pond.

Hint

- Collect and save things all year long for the Nature Garden.

Seeds and Weeds

fresh or dry flowers
leaves
nuts
pinecones
rocks
seed pods
thistles
twigs

age 3 & up

easy prep

help needed

Pressed Play Clay

Art Process

1. Cut Plexiglas into 10" x 10" (25 cm x 25 cm) or smaller pieces.
2. Place one sheet of Plexiglas on the floor.
3. Place little balls and blobs of colored play clay on the sheet of plastic. Place them randomly or make a design, such as a flower shape. (Small bits and pinches of clay work best.)
4. Gently place the second sheet of clear plastic on top of the clay design.
5. Kneel over the project and press the sheet of plastic down. Watch the colored clay squish, spread, flaten, and blend together.
6. Twist, rock, or squish, if desired.
7. Secure the two sheets of plastic together with wide, silver duct tape. Put tape around all four edges to make a silver frame.
8. If desired, unbend a large, heavy paper clip and insert it through the duct tape to create a hook to hang the picture.

Materials

scissors
2 sheets of clear, plastic Plexiglas
play clay (Plasticene), in a variety of colors
duct tape
large paper clip, optional

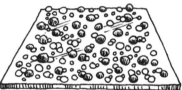

Variation

- Place blobs and drops of paint on a piece of paper. Press a sheet of Plexiglas on the painted paper and watch the design smear, squish, blur, swirl, and blend. Peel off the plastic to reveal a pressed paint design on the paper.

Hints

- Use Plexiglas that is fairly strong and thick ($1/16$" to $1/8$" thick) so it won't snap or break when artists press on it.
- To help prevent the Plexiglas from cracking during the pressing stage, engage lots of helping hands and use little balls and pinches of clay.
- Instead of saving the pressed clay design, peel the Plexiglas sheets apart, scrape the clay off, and use it again.

BIND THE TWO PIECES WITH SILVER DUCT-TAPE...

Plastic Bag Art

Materials

plaster of Paris
spoon
plastic sandwich bag
tablespoon
powdered tempera
   paint
water
tempera paint and
   paintbrushes,
   optional
glue, optional
wooden block or
   piece of matte
   board, optional

Art Process

1. Scoop plaster of Paris
    into a plastic sandwich bag.
2. Add 1 tablespoon (20 g) powdered
    tempera paint to the plaster.
3. Pour in enough water to form a soft
    dough.
4. Squeeze the plastic bag to mix the
    water, paint, and plaster. As soon as you
    feel the plaster becoming warm, it is
    beginning to set. (It will set quickly!)

SQUEEZE TO MIX!

5. As the plaster hardens, mold the bag into a shape.
6. When the sculpture is hard, remove it from the bag.
7. If desired, paint it with tempera paint.
8. Glue the sculpture to a base, such as a wooden block or a piece of matte
    board, if desired.

Hint

• Experiment using different measurements of plaster and water. A half bag
  of plaster and ¼ cup (60 ml) water is a good amount to use.

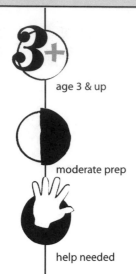

age 3 & up

moderate prep

help needed

Frozen Balloons

Art Process

1. Fill balloons with water and tie knots in their openings.
2. Place the balloons on a cookie sheet and put them in the freezer for two days.
3. Remove the balloons from the freezer.
4. Tear the balloons and remove them from the ice balloons.
5. Fill a large tub with water and place the frozen balloons in it.
6. Using eyedroppers, drop food coloring or watercolor paints onto the frozen balloons.
7. Push, float, and manipulate the balloons into various designs and patterns.

Materials

balloons, all shapes and sizes
water
cookie sheet
freezer
large tub
eyedroppers
food coloring or
    watercolor paints

Variations

- Drop colored salty water on the frozen balloons and watch what happens.
- Fill the balloons with colored water before freezing them.
- Freeze water in other types of containers, bags, or molds and add the frozen shapes to the floating ice sculpture.
- Fill the balloons with tempera paint thinned with water. "Paint" on a piece of paper using the frozen balloons.

Hint

- Artists will enjoy standing around the tub watching the colors mix and swirl, and the ice balloons floating, sinking, and bumping into each other.

Applesauce Cinnamon Dough

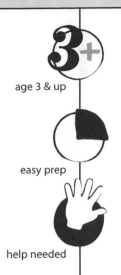
Materials

strainer
coffee filter
applesauce
measuring spoons
cinnamon
bowl
rolling pin
cookie cutters
drinking straw
cooling rack or wax
paper
yarn or ribbon

Art Process

1. Line a strainer with a coffee filter.
2. Pour applesauce into the strainer and let it drain overnight.
3. Mix 10 tablespoons (150 g) cinnamon and 5 tablespoons (100 g) drained applesauce together in a bowl to form a dough. (Hint: If the dough is too wet, add more cinnamon; too dry, add more applesauce.)
4. Place the dough on the work surface and flatten it using a rolling pin.
5. Cut out cookie cutter shapes.
6. To create hanging shapes, use a drinking straw to cut a hole into each shape.
7. Place shapes on a cooling rack or wax paper to dry.
8. The next day, turn the shapes over to allow their backs to dry.
9. Tie a piece of yarn or ribbon through the hole and hang the shapes.

5 TBSP. APPLESAUCE   10 TBSP. CINNAMON

MIX TOGETHER TO FORM DOUGH

Variations

- Dry shapes using a food dehydrator.
- Form shapes using your fingers instead of cookie cutters.
- Cut free-form objects using scissors or a knife.

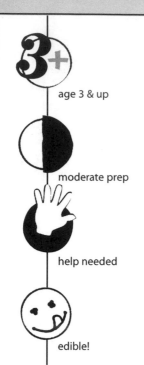

age 3 & up

moderate prep

help needed

edible!

Jacko-Cheese

MIX WITH CLEAN HANDS!

2 CUPS CHEESE

1/4 C. FLOUR

2 TBSP. MAYONNAISE

Materials
measuring cups
   and spoons
cheese grater
cheddar cheese
bowl
flour
mayonnaise
wax paper
plastic knife, toothpick, and other kitchen tools

Art Process

1. Grate 2 cups (250 g) cheddar cheese into a bowl.
2. Add ¼ cup (30 g) flour and 2 tablespoons (40 g) mayonnaise to the cheese.
3. Use your hands to squeeze and blend the ingredients until it has a dough-like consistency. If the dough is too sticky, add more flour; if it is too stiff or dry, add more cheese or mayonnaise.
4. Place a ball of cheese dough on a square of wax paper or a clean work surface.
5. Mold, pat, and sculpt the cheese dough into a flattened oval or circle (resembling a pumpkin).
6. Using a plastic knife or other kitchen tool, cut out holes for the pumpkin's face.
7. Leave the jacko-face on the wax paper square and save it in the refrigerator to eat later.
8. Make as many cheese sculptures or faces as desired.

Variation

• Make little cheese ghosts with faces using white cheddar cheese or Monterey Jack cheese.

Hint

• When using food for art projects, make it part of a meal or a nutritious snack.

PAT INTO A "PUMPKIN"

Sugar Mint Modeling

Materials

measuring cups and spoons
butter or margarine
light corn syrup
peppermint extract
salt
1 box of powdered sugar
large bowl
spoons
small bowls
food coloring

Art Process

1. Mix ⅓ cup (80 g) butter or margarine, ⅓ cup (80 ml) light corn syrup, 1 teaspoon (5 ml) peppermint extract, ½ teaspoon (3 g) salt, and 1 pound (600 g) powdered sugar in a large bowl.
2. Divide the mixture and place it into small bowls, 1 for each color desired.
3. Stir drops of food coloring into each of the bowls.
4. Create designs and sculptures using the Sugar Mint mixture. Combine and mix colors too.
5. Eat and enjoy your creations.

Variations

- Experiment using other flavorings such as almond, vanilla, or lemon.
- Wrap the finished sculptures in cellophane or plastic wrap, tie them with a bow, and give them as gifts.

Hints

- Artists' fingers and faces can get very sticky (surprise!) with this project. Warm little hands will soften the dough substantially, which makes it quite sticky.
- Sculptures will harden somewhat if refrigerated.
- Sugar Mint Sculptures are very, very sweet.

MOLD DESIGNS!

age 3 & up

involved prep

help needed

edible!

Candy Clay

Art Process

1. Using your hands, mix ⅓ cup (80 g) butter or margarine, ⅓ cup (80 ml) light corn syrup, ½ teaspoon (3 g) salt, and 1 teaspoon (5 ml) vanilla in a bowl.
2. Pour in 1 pound (600 g) powdered sugar. Knead the dough until smooth.
3. If necessary, add more powdered sugar to make the clay non-sticky and more pliable.
4. Divide the clay into small portions and mix in food colors or paste food dye. Use a spatula or spreading knife to mix the colors.
5. Place bits of colored candy clay on a paper towel and decorate a plain graham cracker.
6. Eat your creation!

EXTRA POWDERED SUGAR

LOVELY
GRAHAM CRACKER.

Variation

• Prepare a butter cream frosting and frost a cake, cupcakes, or graham crackers. Then, place the candy clay designs on top of the frosting.

Hints

• This recipe makes enough candy clay for thirty artists to decorate one graham cracker or cupcake, or for one artist to decorate thirty crackers or cupcakes.
• Avoid making candy clay on a hot day because the butter will melt and make the clay too sticky.
• Make flat figures and designs to achieve the best results.

Apple Heart Pizza

Materials

large mixing bowl
measuring cups and
  spoons
flour
butter
sugar
salt
cold water
cutting board
rolling pin
spatula
cookie sheet
apple peeler/corer
3 medium-sized
  apples
knife
medium bowl
cinnamon
oven
plate

Art Process—The Crust

1. In a large mixing bowl, combine 2 ¼ cups (280 g) flour and 1 ¼ sticks (310 g) butter at room temperature. Use your hands to mix them together until the flour turns yellow.
2. Blend in 3 tablespoons (60 g) sugar and ¼ teaspoon (1 g) salt.
3. Pour in ¼ cup (60 ml) cold water and continue to blend with your fingers until the dough forms a ball.
4. Sprinkle flour onto a cutting board. Place the dough on the floured board and knead for 5 minutes. Add more flour if needed.
5. Shape the dough into a ball and divide it into four equal pieces.
6. Use a rolling pin to roll each piece about ¼" (6 mm) thick. Sprinkle flour on the dough to prevent it from sticking.
7. Mold each piece into a flat heart shape. Slide a spatula under the shapes and place them on a cookie sheet. Repeat for all three pieces.

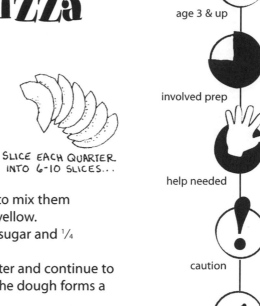

SLICE EACH QUARTER INTO 6-10 SLICES...

Art Process—The Apple Pizza

1. Core and peel three medium-sized apples.
2. Cut each apple into four quarters. Slice each quarter into six to ten pieces and place them in a medium bowl.
3. Sprinkle 1 teaspoon (6 g) sugar and ½ teaspoon (1 g) cinnamon over the apple slices and toss until the apples are evenly coated.
4. Place the apple slices on each dough heart, in a pinwheel shape or other design.
5. Turn the oven to 400° F, place the baking sheet into it, and bake for 15 minutes (until the edges are golden brown).
6. Remove the baking sheet from the oven and slide the pizzas onto a plate. Eat them hot, warm, or cool!

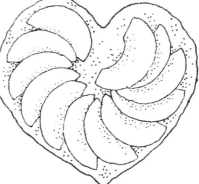

ARRANGE APPLE SLICES AND BAKE!

Hint

- To save time, roll out the dough ahead of time, cover it, and store it in the refrigerator until artists are ready to add the apples and bake.

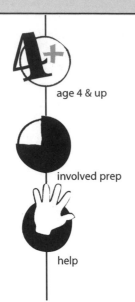

age 4 & up

involved prep

help

Fairy Dust Glitter Gel

Materials
measuring cups and
   spoons
aloe vera gel
glycerin
small bowl
rubber spatula
fine polyester glitter,
   any color
fragrance oil
food coloring

Art Process
1. Mix ¼ cup (60 ml) aloe and 1 teaspoon (5 ml) glycerin in a small bowl.
2. Stir in glitter, 5 drops of fragrance oil, and 1 drop of food coloring.
3. Use the gel immediately. This is a fun, whimsical gel that you can dab or spread on your skin. Use it whenever you want to add shine and sparkle to your cheeks, shoulders, or arms.

Hint
- Purchase fine polyester glitter at most craft stores.

MIX ¼ CUP ALOE AND 1 tsp. GLYCERIN...

FOOD COLOR 1 DROP   GLITTER
FRAGRANCE OIL 5 DROPS

STIR IN THESE INGREDIENTS.

Dryer Lint Clay

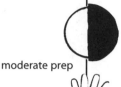

moderate prep

help needed

Materials

measuring cups and
   spoons
dryer lint
bowl
warm water
white glue
clear dishwashing
   liquid

Art Process

1. Tear 2 cups (60 g) firmly packed dryer lint into
   little bits.
2. Place the lint in a bowl and mix in $1/3$ cup (80 ml)
   warm water, 6 tablespoons (90 ml) white glue,
   and 1 tablespoon (15 ml) clear dishwashing
   liquid.
3. Knead the clay to make it pliable.
4. Create clay shapes or forms.
5. Allow objects to dry for several days before
   painting, stringing, or otherwise handling them.

TEAR UP THE LINT
INTO TINY BITS.

2 CUPS
DRYER LINT

1 TBSP.
CLEAR
DISHWASHING
LIQUID

6 TBSP.
WHITE GLUE

$1/3$ CUP
WARM
WATER

MIX IN THESE
INGREDIENTS

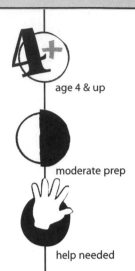

age 4 & up

moderate prep

help needed

Claydoh Beads

Materials

measuring cups
flour
cornstarch
salt
bowl
powdered tempera
paint or
    vegetable dye,
    optional
warm water
toothpicks
paint and
    paintbrushes,
    optional
clear gloss enamel,
    optional
string, yarn, or
    leather cords

Art Process

1. Mix ³/₄ cup (90 g) flour, ¹/₂ cup (60 g) cornstarch, and ¹/₂ cup (100 g) salt in a bowl.
2. If desired, add powdered tempera paint or vegetable dye to make colored dough.
3. Slowly pour in ³/₈ cup (90 ml) warm water and knead the mixture into a stiff dough.
4. Add flour to reduce stickiness, if necessary.
5. Roll pieces of dough into balls to form beads.
6. Poke a toothpick through each ball to make a hole.
7. Allow the beads to dry for a few days. (Large beads take longer to dry.)
8. Paint the dry beads, if desired. Coat the beads with clear gloss enamel to add shine, if desired.
9. When the beads are dry, string them on yarn, string, or leather cords. Knots tied between beads will prevent the beads from slipping.

ADD SLOWLY....

Hints

- To dry the beads, stick toothpicks into a ball of playdough. Then, place a bead onto each toothpick.
- Twist the beads on the toothpicks as they dry to prevent them from sticking to the toothpick.
- This recipe makes a fairly smooth dough that holds its color when dry.
- A bit of salt residue will appear in the beads, especially in darker colored dough.

Salt Ceramic

4+

age 4 & up

moderate prep

help needed

caution

Materials

pan
stove or hot plate
measuring cups
salt
cornstarch
water
wooden spoon
aluminum foil
feathers, toothpicks, pebbles, or other objects

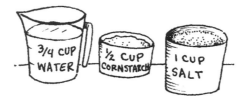

COOK THESE THREE INGREDIENTS OVER MEDIUM HEAT. STIR CONSTANTLY!

Art Process

1. Place a pan on the stove and mix in 1 cup (250 g) salt, ½ cup (60 g) cornstarch, and ¾ cup (180 ml) water.
2. Cook the mixture over medium heat (supervise closely), stirring constantly until it thickens into a big, white glob. (One batch of this recipe makes a ball the size of a large orange.)
3. Remove the mixture from the heat and place it on a piece of foil to cool.
4. After the mixture has cooled, knead it thoroughly until it is soft and pliable.
5. Sculpt objects or designs.
6. Insert feathers, toothpicks, pebbles, or other embellishments while the ceramic is still soft.
7. This material will dry rock hard without baking.

Variations

- Brush a clear glaze or fingernail polish over the finished dry object to make it shiny.
- Make pendants; beads; figures; letters; holiday decorations; items to glue on plaques; or play fruit, vegetables, and cookies.

Hints

- Add paste food coloring or liquid tempera to the mixture to make colored dough.
- Store leftover Salt Ceramic in a plastic bag; it will keep for a few days. Knead the dough before using to restore softness.

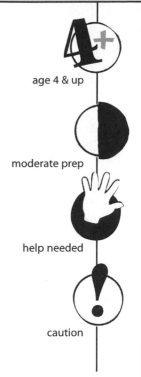

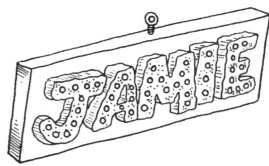

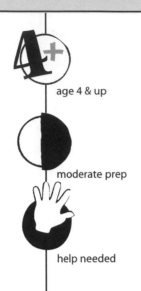

age 4 & up

moderate prep

help needed

Diamond Crystal Treasures

Art Process

1. Make a first batch to resemble diamonds. Mix 1 cup (300 g) rock salt and ¼ cup (60 ml) glue in a bowl. Using a rubber spatula, stir for several minutes until it is thick.
2. Form "diamonds" from this mix by hand.
3. Place globs of diamond crystals on a sheet of wax paper.
4. Allow the crystals to dry overnight. The longer they dry, the clearer the glue will be and the more crystal-clear the "diamonds" will become.
5. Make another batch with food coloring. Make red rubies, green emeralds, or blue sapphires. Mix the salt and food coloring, then add the glue.
6. Stir the mixture.
7. Squeeze globs of crystal jewels onto a piece of wax paper. Allow them to dry overnight.
8. Make as many batches of treasures as desired, using various food coloring.

Variations

- Make a treasure chest out of a small cardboard box and fill it with crystal treasures!
- Host a treasure hunt.

Materials
measuring cups
white glue
rock salt
small bowls
rubber spatula
wax paper
food coloring

Stomped Foil Sculpture

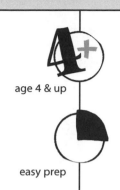
Materials

aluminum foil, new
or recycled
masking tape
matte board, black
or other color

Art Process

1. Squeeze or squash a piece of aluminum foil into a ball or other shape.
2. Place the foil shape on the floor and stomp on it until it is completely flat.
3. Tear off pieces of masking tape, fold them into loops, and place them on the backs of the flattened foil.
4. Press the flattened foil on a piece of matte board. If necessary, add more tape.

Variations

• Paint or color the matte board to create a colorful background for the stomped sculpture.

• Tie black thread to the Stomped Foil Sculpture and suspend it from the ceiling.

Hint

• This project is an exhilarating art experience for artists of any age.

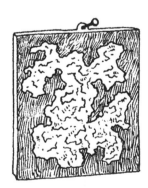

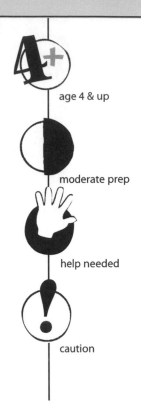

age 4 & up

moderate prep

help needed

caution

Painted Foil Sculpture

Materials
tacky glue
tempera paint
liquid detergent
spoon
bowl
aluminum foil,
   recycled or new
matte board or
   cardboard
glue gun, optional
paintbrush

Art Process
1. Mix tacky glue with tempera paint and a few drops of liquid detergent to make glue paint.
2. Mold a piece of foil into a shape or sculpture.
3. Mount the sculpture onto a piece of matte board using tacky glue or glue paint. Or, ask an adult to use a glue gun to stick the foil shape to the matte board.
4. Allow plenty of time for the glue to dry.
5. Paint the sculpture using the glue paint. (Glue paint will allow the silver color of the foil to shine through.)

Variations
• To make the glue paint more transparent, mix food coloring into the glue. To make it more opaque, add more tempera paint.
• Attach wood scraps or other collage and sculpture materials to the foil sculpture.

Hints
• Aluminum foil is a wonderful art medium, and it is inexpensive and convenient. Encourage artists to experiment and explore. Recycle or reuse first attempts.
• It is difficult to make detailed features, extensions, or body parts with foil.
• Try to make sculptures using one piece of foil.

Tissue Mâché

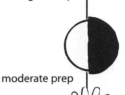

age 4 & up

moderate prep

help needed

Materials
facial tissues, white
    or colored
bowl or bucket
liquid starch
liquid glue
paint and paint-
    brushes, optional

Art Process
1. Tear facial tissues into pieces or strips and place them in a bowl or bucket.
2. Add just enough liquid starch to cover the tissues.
3. Allow the tissues to soak in the starch until they are mushy.
4. Add liquid glue to the tissue pulp until it holds a form. If it is too squishy, add more tissue.
5. Squeeze out excess starch.
6. Shape and mold the tissue mâché.
7. Allow the shapes to dry and paint them, if desired.

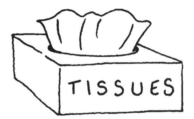

Variations
• Cover a form, such as a balloon, milk carton, plastic liter bottle, or balls of newspaper, with the tissue mâché.
• Substitute toilet paper for facial tissue.

ADD GLUE UNTIL PULP HOLDS A FORM...

POUR JUST ENOUGH STARCH TO COVER.

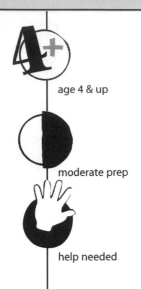

age 4 & up

moderate prep

help needed

Tissue Mobile

Art Process

1. Cut a piece of yarn 1 yard (1 m) long and tie the ends together.
2. Mix 2 parts white glue to 1 part liquid starch in a cup.
3. Dip the yarn into the cup of glue mixture. Squeeze out the excess glue by running your fingers down the yarn.
4. Place the sticky yarn in any design on a piece of art tissue or white tissue.
5. Cover the piece of yarn with another piece of tissue and gently press it down.
6. Allow the project to dry overnight.
7. The next day, cut out the yarn shape. If desired, paint the shape using watercolors.
8. Make a loop to hang the Tissue Mobile using a needle and thread.
9. Hang one or more of these shapes from a coat hanger. Painted shapes can dry directly on the coat hanger.

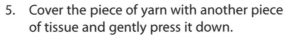

Materials

yarn
scissors
white glue
liquid starch
cup
spoon
art tissue or white tissue
paintbrushes and watercolor paints, optional
needle
thread
coat hanger

Variations

- Use this project to make holiday ornaments.
- Hang the mobile in a window to let light shine through it.

Hint

- When squeezing excess glue from the yarn, pull gently. If the artist pulls too hard, the yarn will stretch, spring out of control, and flip glue everywhere.

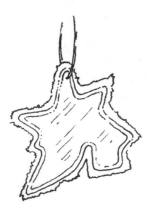

PRESS GENTLY
WHERE YARN TOUCHES PAPER...

String Thing

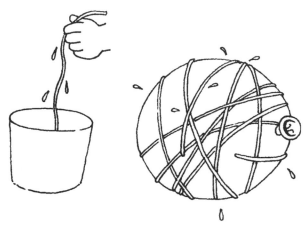

Materials

measuring spoons
   and cups
granulated starch
water
pan
stove or hot plate
spoon
bowl
balloon
yarn or embroidery
   floss
scissors
thread

Art Process

1. Make an extra strong liquid starch mixture by dissolving additional granulated starch into the amount of water recommended on the package (supervise closely). Follow the rest of the instructions on the package.
2. Place the mixture into a bowl and allow it to cool.
3. Blow up a balloon and tie a knot at the end (supervise closely).
4. Cut yarn or embroidery floss into pieces no longer than 1 yard (1 m).
5. Dip a piece of string into the starch mixture and completely cover it with starch. Wring out the string to make it less heavy.
6. Wrap the string around the balloon, making sure to plaster down the ends.
7. Cover the balloon with string, but do not completely conceal it.
8. Allow the project to dry overnight. When the string is thoroughly dry, pop the balloon and remove it.
9. Tie a piece of thread to the String Thing and hang it from the ceiling, a branch, or some other framework.

Hints

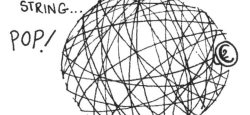

STICK
A PIN
BETWEEN
STRING...

POP!

- Artists have a tendency to overwrap their balloons. If they use too much string, it will slip off the balloon into a pile. If this happens, begin again and use less string.
- Gently squeeze the yarn between two fingers to remove some of the starch. The yarn will remain sticky, but it won't be too heavy.

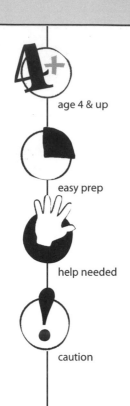

age 4 & up

easy prep

help needed

caution

Paper Bag Sculpture

Art Process

1. Fill a paper bag with wads of newspaper. Shape the bag into a form to make the base of the sculpture.
2. Cut or tear strips of newspaper and dip them into the papier-mâché paste (see recipe).
3. Pick up a strip, wring out the excess paste, and wrap it around the paper bag base.
4. Continue wringing out strips and adding them to the base, forming details such as arms, a tail, or handles.
5. Allow the sculpture to dry overnight. (In moist weather, drying may take two days.)
6. When the sculpture is completely dry, paint it using tempera paints.

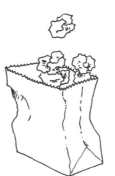

Materials

paper bags, any size
newspaper
scissors, optional
wheat paste or homemade paste (see recipe)
tempera paints
paintbrushes

Variation

• Cover other forms with with papier-mâché, including cardboard boxes, milk cartons, or meat trays.

Hints

• Wring out newspaper strips by pulling them between two fingers.
• Paper bags are easier than balloons for young artists to control.
• Use wheat paste or wallpaper paste instead of homemade paste, if desired. They work just as well and are available in bulk containers at hardware stores.

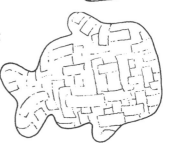

IT COULD BE A FISH....

OR A MONSTER!

Homemade Paste for Papier-mâché

pan
stove or hot plate
cold water
measuring cups
flour
spoon
peppermint oil, optional

Place a pan on top of the stove and pour in 3 cups (720 ml) cold water. Stir in 1½ cups (190 g) flour and cook the mixture over low heat until it thickens to a creamy, paste-like consistency. Add more water if it is too thick. Allow the paste to cool. Add a few drops of peppermint oil.

Bowling

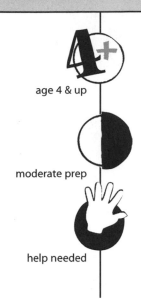

age 4 & up

moderate prep

help needed

Materials
funnel
plastic juice bottles
sand or rice
newspaper
wallpaper paste
paint
paintbrushes
yarn
white glue
college materials,
   optional
clear gloss enamel
   or polymer
masking tape
soft balls

Art Process
1. Use a funnel to fill each plastic bottle about ⅓ full with sand or rice.
2. Crumple a full page of newspaper into a round shape (like a head). Pull out a small section to make a neck. Insert the neck into the bottle, with the head sticking out.
3. Tear pages of newspaper into strips.
4. Coat the newspaper strips with wallpaper paste and paste them over the head, down the neck, and all over the entire bottle.
5. Allow the project to dry for several days.
6. Paint facial features onto the bottles, such as eyes, a nose, and a mouth. Glue yarn on the head to make hair. Or, if desired, paint brightly colored designs on the bottle or decorate it using collage materials. Allow the paint to dry completely.
7. Paint the bowling bottle using clear gloss enamel or polymer. Allow the gloss to dry.
8. Now you are ready to bowl! Set up the bottles at the end of a room and mark the floor (like an alley) with masking tape. Roll soft balls or any other balls down the alley and see how many bottles you can knock over.

Hints
- Filling the bottles with sand or rice will prevent them from tipping over too easily.
- Keep in mind that the bottles can lose their "heads," the paint may chip off, or other disasters may occur if the artists throw the balls too hard or if the alley is too long. Most children will naturally overdo their throwing, so start small.

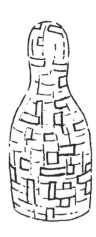

age 4 & up

involved prep

help needed

caution

edible!

Stained Glass Cookies

Art Process

1. Add $\frac{1}{2}$ teaspoon (2 g) baking soda to 3 cups (375 g) flour.
2. Using your hands, mix $\frac{1}{3}$ cup (80 g) vegetable shortening, $\frac{1}{3}$ cup (80 g) sugar, 1 egg, 3 cups (375 g) flour (mixed with baking soda), $\frac{2}{3}$ cup (360 g) honey, and 1 teaspoon (7 g) salt in a bowl.
3. Roll the dough into $\frac{1}{4}$" (6 mm) thick snake-like shapes.
4. Cover a cookie sheet with aluminum foil.
5. Make outlines of shapes, such as hearts, circles, cars, birds, faces, or other objects. Make sure to connect the ends of the dough rolls together.
6. Place shapes on the cookie sheet.
7. Crush multi-colored lollipops or hard candy into small pieces.
8. Sprinkle the crushed candy into the spaces of the cookies, completely filling them.
9. Turn the oven to 375° F, place the cookie sheet in the oven, and bake for 8 to 10 minutes.
10. Remove the cookies from the oven and allow them to cool.
11. When the cookies are cool and firm, gently peel them from the aluminum foil.
12. Eat and enjoy your delicious Stained Glass Cookies!

Hint

- Experiment using different colors of crushed candy. (Red always seems to be a favorite.)

Materials

measuring cups and spoons
baking soda
flour
vegetable shortening
sugar
1 egg
honey
salt
bowl
aluminum foil
cookie sheet
lollipops or hard candies
oven

Edible Sculpting Dough

age 4 & up

involved prep

help needed

caution

edible!

Materials

dry yeast
measuring cups and
    spoons
very warm water
bowl and spoon
1 egg
honey
shortening
salt
flour
large cutting board
baking sheet
towel
oven

Art Process

1. Mix 1 package of yeast and 1½ cups (360 ml) very warm water in a bowl.
2. Add 1 egg, ¼ cup (90 ml) honey, ¼ cup (60 g) shortening, and 1 teaspoon (7 g) salt to the mixture.
3. Slowly mix in 5 cups (625 g) flour, forming a ball of dough. Add more flour if the dough is too sticky.
4. Sprinkle flour onto a large cutting board and place the ball of dough on it.
5. Knead the dough. Sculpt flat figures (since the dough will rise).
6. Place the sculptures on a baking sheet and cover them with a towel.
7. Move the baking sheet to a warm place to let the dough rise (about ½ hour). To make puffy sculptures, let the dough rise for a longer period of time.
8. Turn the oven to 350° F.
9. Remove the towel from the cookie sheet and place the sculptures in the oven. Bake them for 20 minutes or until they are golden brown. Eat and enjoy your sculptures. Or save them, if desired.

ADD THESE INGREDIENTS...

¼ CUP HONEY   ¼ CUP SHORTENING

1 tsp. SALT

Variation

*   Create a hanging sculpture. Insert a paper clip into the dough sculpture before baking. After the cookie is cool, loop yarn, ribbon, or colorful embroidery floss through the paper clip and hang it from a tree, nail, or doorknob.

SLOWLY ADD FLOUR...

age 4 & up

involved prep

help needed

edible!

Royal Icing Art

Art Process

1. Place an egg white into a small bowl and beat until stiff.
2. Add 1¼ cups (190 g) sifted powdered sugar, 1 tablespoon at a time. Beat the mixture after each addition.
3. When the icing is thick and spreadable, add ½ teaspoon (2 ml) lemon juice. (This will help the icing dry more quickly.)
4. Cover a piece of cardboard with aluminum foil.
5. Place a few of the yummy decorations (see list) onto the cardboard. Using the icing as cement or glue, stick cookies and sweets together to make animals, toys, or holiday scenes. Use pipe cleaners as decorations, if desired.
6. Eat your creations right away or display them.

Materials

1 egg white
small bowl
egg beater or
   electric mixer
measuring cups and
   spoons
powdered sugar
lemon juice
cardboard or a pizza
   cardboard circle
aluminum foil
yummy decorations
   (see list)
spreading knives
pipe cleaners,
   optional

Variation

· Make cookie houses; a barn-yard scene, with a marshmal-low pig and cookie fence; a Santa face with a white icing beard and jelly bean nose; or a ski scene with toy skiers on icing hills

Yummy Decorations

candies
cookies
marshmallows
shredded coconut
sprinkles

Hints

· Double or triple this recipe, if desired. However, when making large batches, keep a damp cloth over the bowl to prevent the icing from drying out.
· Store excess icing in airtight containers in the refrigerator for up to a week.

Marzipan Fantasy Fruits

ages 4 & up

involved prep

help needed

edible!

Materials

marzipan
food coloring
sliced almonds
cloves
airtight containers
   or plastic wrap

Art Process

1. Place marzipan on the work surface and break it into several balls.
2. Add a few drops of food coloring to each ball and use your hands to work the coloring into the marzipan.
3. Create real or imaginary fruits, or any shapes and designs.
4. Add sliced almonds to form leaves and cloves to form stems.
5. Store marzipan fantasy fruits in airtight containers or cover them with plastic wrap.

Variations

- Make sculptures such as balloons, clowns, animals, flowers, or abstract shapes instead of fruits.
- Give finished designs as gifts for various holidays.
- Use marzipan fruits to decorate cakes or desserts.

Hints

- The Fantasy Fruits are edible; however, most children don't seem to like the flavor of marzipan.
- Marzipan is available at bakeries, grocery stores, candy stores, and cake baking supply stores.

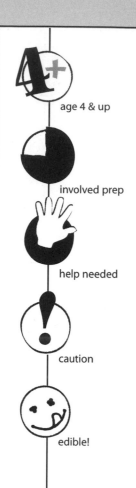

age 4 & up

involved prep

help needed

caution

edible!

Bread Sculpture

1 tsp SUGAR

1 TBSP YEAST

Art Process

1. Mix 1 cup (240 ml) warm water, 1 teaspoon (7 g) sugar, and 1 tablespoon (20 g) or 1 package of dry yeast in a bowl until the yeast softens (about 2 to 3 minutes).

2. Add 1 cup (125 g) flour to the dough and stir vigorously with a wooden spoon. Stir the mixture until it is smooth.

3. Add 1 tablespoon (15 ml) oil, 1 teaspoon (7 g) salt, and another cup (125 g) of flour to the dough.

4. Sprinkle flour onto a cutting board and pour the thick batter onto it.

5. Slowly add more flour while kneading the dough. (Keep a coating of flour on the dough to prevent sticking.) Knead the dough for about 5 minutes, until it is smooth, elastic, and satiny. (If you poke a finger into the dough, the dough should bounce back.)

6. Coat a bowl with a layer of oil and place the dough in it. Cover the bowl with a towel and place it in a warm area for about 45 minutes to let the dough rise.

7. Remove the towel from the bowl. Punch the dough down and work it into a smooth ball. Divide the dough into separate portions and create dough sculptures.

8. Place the dough sculptures on a baking sheet, turn the oven to 400° F, and place the sheet in the lower part of the oven.

9. Bake the dough sculptures for 15 to 20 minutes, or until they are golden. (Large forms may take longer.) Remove dough sculptures from the oven and cool them on a rack.

THEN ADD...

1 TBSP. OIL

1 tsp. SALT

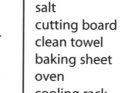

THEN ADD A SECOND CUP OF FLOUR!

BEAT VIGOROUSLY!

Materials

measuring cups and
  spoons
warm water
sugar
dry yeast
mixing bowls
flour
wooden spoon
oil
salt
cutting board
clean towel
baking sheet
oven
cooling rack

Hints

• Bread dough sculptures are great to make for holidays.
• Keep a small bowl of flour handy for artists to dip their hands. Young artists sometimes prefer playing with the soft flour instead of making sculptures.

Candy Bugs

age 5 & up

involved prep

help needed

edible!

Materials
small candy pieces
dried fruits
clear plastic wrap
pipe cleaners, rubber bands, strings, or ribbons
toothpicks, optional

Art Process

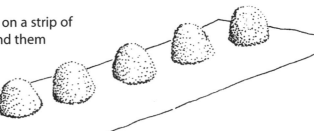

1. Place candy pieces and dried fruits on a strip of plastic wrap. Wind the plastic around them to form a caterpillar or another insect shape.
2. Twist pipe cleaners between the pieces of candy or at appropriate intervals to form the head, body, and legs of the insect.
3. If desired, use toothpicks to make spines, antennae, stingers, or teeth.
4. Eat your Candy Bugs. Or, give them out as birthday party favors.

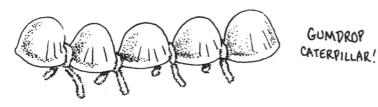

GUMDROP CATERPILLAR!

Hints
- When working with delicious ingredients like candy, it is a good idea to have some extra available for nibbling.
- Plastic wrap can be difficult to control, so keep the pieces small or help artists with the wrapping step.

age 5 & up

easy prep

help needed

caution

Soap Sculpture

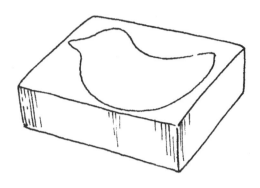

Materials
pen
bar of soap
small knife or other
  sculpting tool,
  such as a spoon,
  toothpick, or
  clay tools
water
cup

Art Process

1. Draw the outline of an object on a bar of soap. (Draw a fairly simple shape without details or intricacies.)
2. Use a knife or other sculpting tool to sculpt and cut away the soap from the design (supervise closely).
3. Pour water into a cup.
4. Dip your finger into the water and rub over the soap to smooth edges and sides.
5. Enjoy the finished design as a sculpture, or use it as a fancy guest soap.

Variation

•   Make Soap Clay (see page 16) and mold or carve it.

FANCY SOAP!

Hints

•   Supervise this project closely.
•   Brace the sculpture while you carve it. For example, place the soap against a block of wood that is nailed into another board.

Wire Sculpting

age 5 & up

involved prep

help needed

Materials

measuring cups
plaster of Paris
water
bowl
spoon
1/2 pint milk cartons
scrap telephone cable
   (colored wires inside the
cable)
scissors or wire snips
decorative items such as beads or ribbon,
   optional
watercolor paints, optional

Art Process

1. Mix 1 cup (125 g) plaster of Paris and ½ cup (120 ml) water in a bowl.
2. Pour the plaster into the ½ pint milk cartons. (It will fill about three cartons.)
3. Cut telephone cable into 12" (30 cm) or smaller pieces.
4. As the plaster begins to harden, place wires into the plaster in any arrangement.
5. Allow the plaster to harden.
6. When the plaster is dry and hard, tear away the milk carton.
7. Bend and sculpt the wires into a shape or sculpture.
8. Add decorative sculpture items to the wires, if desired.
9. Paint the plaster with watercolors, if desired.

MODERN ART!

Hints

- Call the local phone company and ask for scrap wire. Strip off the outer covering to reveal a rainbow of wires.
- Never rinse plaster down the drain because it can harden in the plumbing and cause big problems. Allow the remaining plaster to harden in a mixing bowl and pop it out when it is dry. Wipe the bowl with a wet towel and wash it in the sink. Wash hands in a bucket of soapy water and discard the water outside.

age 5 & up

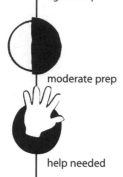

moderate prep

help needed

Scrimshaw Pendant

Materials

measuring cups
water
large measuring cup
plaster of Paris
large spoon
wax paper
toothpick, nail,
   or pin
markers
rag
shellac, optional
leather thong

Art Process

1. Pour ²⁄₃ cup (160 ml) water into a large measuring cup. Mix in 1 cup (125 g) plaster of Paris and stir until the mixture is thick and smooth. (Remember to work fast because plaster hardens quickly.)
2. Drop a spoonful of plaster onto a piece of wax paper. If necessary, use the back of a spoon to smooth it down.
3. Poke a hole into the top of the plaster blob (with a toothpick) while it is still soft.
4. Allow the plaster to harden for 5-10 minutes.
5. Scratch a design into the plaster using a nail or pin. Try etching a design just like whalers did on shark teeth, whale bones, and walrus tusks.
6. Draw over the scratched design with markers and then use a rag to rub away the excess color. The color will fill in the scratches.
7. Draw additional designs and pictures on the plaster, if desired.
8. Coat the pendant with shellac, if desired, to preserve the design.
9. Thread a leather thong through the hole and wear the plaster scrimshaw as a pendant or necklace.

Hint

- Young artists sometimes make very large pendants—VERY large—but will enjoy wearing them anyway.

A LOVELY PENDANT FOR SAILING!

Salt Figures

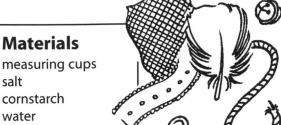

Materials

measuring cups
salt
cornstarch
water
saucepan
wooden spoon
stove or hot plate
aluminum foil
cardboard tube or
    empty frozen juice
    can
food coloring
tooth picks
decorating materials
    (see list)
glue or tape

Art Process

1. Mix 1 cup (250 g) salt, ½ cup (60 g) cornstarch, and ¾ cup (180 ml) water in a saucepan.
2. Place the saucepan over medium heat on the stove. Stir the mixture using a wooden spoon until it thickens into a ball (supervise closely).
3. Remove the mixture from the heat and place it on a piece of foil to cool.
4. Knead the dough thoroughly.
5. Fill a cardboard tube with the clay (or another heavy material) to prevent it from tipping over.
6. Place a ball of clay on top of the tube to make a head.
7. Form small balls of clay and mix food coloring into them. Add facial features using the colored clay. If the features won't stick, moisten them with a bit of water and then attach. Or, use toothpicks to help the features stick to the clay.
8. Allow the project to dry for several days.
9. Glue or tape decorating materials to the Salt Figure to make clothing, hair, hats, glasses, arms, or braids.

Hints

- Knead salt ceramic clay often to keep it smooth and pliable.
- Store clay in an airtight plastic bag until you are ready to use it.

Decorating Materials

colored paper
cotton
fabric trims
feathers
felt
lace
scraps of fabric
yarn

age 5 & up

involved prep

help needed

Paste Batik

Art Process

1. Combine ½ cup (60 g) flour, ½ cup (120 ml) water, and 2 teaspoons (10 g) alum into a blender and blend to form a paste.
2. Pour the paste into several squeeze bottles.
3. Cut a piece of muslin to fit a square of cardboard. Tape the muslin to the cardboard square.
4. Draw on the muslin using the squeeze bottles of paste. Try to maintain a smooth flow of paste and form dots, lines, and solid masses.
5. Allow the project to dry overnight.
6. Mix paste food colors with water in shallow tin cans. (A small amount will provide a rich hue.)
7. Dip a paintbrush into the food color mixture and brush colors over the dry paste designs.
8. After the project is dry, chip and rub the dry paste off the muslin using your fingers. The drawing underneath will be white.

Materials

measuring cups and
   spoons
flour
water
alum
blender
several squeeze
   bottles
tape
scissors
small piece of 100%
   cotton muslin,
   unlaundered
corrugated
   cardboard
paste food color
water
shallow cans
paintbrushes

FOOD COLOR MIX

Variation

• Make a greeting card by gluing the batik to a piece of colored paper.

Hints

• Shallow tuna or pineapple cans are more stable than tall containers for holding the paste food coloring.
• A large 3′ x 5′ (1 m x 1.5 m) piece of muslin works well for a group project.

Index

Indexes

Icons index
    Preparation
    Help
    Caution
    Edible!
    Ages
Alphabetical Index of
    Activities
Materials Index

Icons Index

Preparation Index

Easy prep

Applesauce Cinnamon
    Dough, 31
Gak (Homemade Silly
    Putty), 10
Nature Garden, 27
Paint Dough, 11
Paper Bag Sculpture, 46
Playdough Car and Track, 25
Pressed Play Clay, 28
Soap Sculpture, 54
Stomped Foil Sculpture, 41

Moderate prep
Bowling, 47
Brick Making, 21
Candle Holder, 26
Claydoh Beads, 38
Cooked Playdough, 14
Craft Clay, 18
Diamond Crystal Treasures, 40
Dryer Lint Clay, 37
Frozen Balloons, 30
Great Goop, 9
Jacko-Cheese, 32
No-Cook Playdough, 13
Painted Foil Sculpture, 42
Peanut Butter Dough, 20
Plastic Bag Art, 29
Playful Clay, 17
Salt Ceramic, 39
Scrimshaw Pendant, 56
Soapy Clay, 16
Squishy Mixture, 12
String Thing, 45

Sugar Mint Modeling, 33
Tissue Mâché, 43
Tissue Mobile, 44
Tutti Frutti Playdough, 15
Yeast Dough, 19

Involved prep

Apple Heart Pizza, 35
Bread Sculpture, 52
Brick Building, 22
Candy Bugs, 53
Candy Clay, 34
Earth Clay Explore, 23
Earth Clay Sculpture, 24
Edible Sculpting Dough, 49
Fairy Dust Glitter Gel, 36
Marzipan Fantasy Fruits, 51
Paste Batik, 58
Royal Icing Art, 50
Salt Figures, 57
Stained Glass Cookies, 48
Wire Sculpting, 55

Some help needed
Apple Heart Pizza, 35
Applesauce Cinnamon
    Dough, 31
Bowling, 47
Bread Sculpture, 52
Brick Making, 21
Candle Holder, 26
Candy Bugs, 53
Candy Clay, 34
Claydoh Beads, 38
Cooked Playdough, 14
Craft Clay, 18
Diamond Crystal Treasures, 40
Dryer Lint Clay, 37
Earth Clay Explore, 23
Earth Clay Sculpture, 24
Edible Sculpting Dough, 49
Fairy Dust Glitter Gel, 36
Frozen Balloons, 30
Gak (Homemade Silly Putty), 10
Great Goop, 9
Jacko-Cheese, 32
Marzipan Fantasy Fruits, 51
No-Cook Playdough, 13
Paint Dough, 11
Painted Foil Sculpture, 42
Paper Bag Sculpture, 46
Paste Batik, 58
Peanut Butter Dough, 20
Plastic Bag Art, 29

Playdough Car and Track, 25
Playful Clay, 17
Pressed Play Clay, 28
Royal Icing Art, 50
Salt Ceramic, 39
Salt Figures, 57
Scrimshaw Pendant, 56
Soap Sculpture, 54
Soapy Clay, 16
Squishy Mixture, 12
Stained Glass Cookies, 48
String Thing, 45
Sugar Mint Modeling, 33
Tissue Mâché, 43
Tissue Mobile, 44
Tutti Frutti Playdough, 15
Wire Sculpting, 55
Yeast Dough, 19

Caution recommended

Apple Heart Pizza, 35
Bread Sculpture, 52
Brick Making, 21
Candle Holder, 26
Cooked Playdough, 14
Craft Clay, 18
Edible Sculpting Dough, 49
Painted Foil Sculpture, 42
Paper Bag Sculpture, 46
Playdough Car and Track, 25
Playful Clay, 17
Salt Ceramic, 39
Salt Figures, 57
Soap Sculpture, 54
Stained Glass Cookies, 48
String Thing, 45
Tutti Frutti Playdough, 15
Yeast Dough, 19

Edible!
Apple Heart Pizza, 35
Bread Sculpture, 52
Candy Bugs, 53
Candy Clay, 34
Edible Sculpting Dough, 49
Jacko-Cheese, 32
Marzipan Fantasy Fruits, 51
Peanut Butter Dough, 20
Royal Icing Art, 50
Stained Glass Cookies, 48
Sugar Mint Modeling, 33
Yeast Dough, 19

Ages Index

All ages
Cooked Playdough, 14
Craft Clay, 18
Gak (Homemade Silly Putty),
    10
Great Goop, 9
No-Cook Playdough, 13
Paint Dough, 11
Peanut Butter Dough, 20
Playful Clay, 17
Soapy Clay, 16
Squishy Mixture, 12
Tutti Frutti Playdough, 15
Yeast Dough, 19

Age 3 & up
Apple Heart Pizza, 35
Applesauce
    Cinnamon Dough, 31
Brick Building, 22
Brick Making, 21
Candle Holder, 26
Candy Clay, 34
Earth Clay Explore, 23
Earth Clay Sculpture, 24
Frozen Balloons, 30
Jacko-Cheese, 32
Nature Garden, 27
Plastic Bag Art, 29
Playdough Car and Track, 25
Pressed Play Clay, 28
Sugar Mint Modeling, 33

Age 4 & up
Bowling, 47
Bread Sculpture, 52
Claydoh Beads, 38
Diamond Crystal Treasures, 40
Dryer Lint Clay, 37
Edible Sculpting Dough, 49
Fairy Dust Glitter Gel, 36
Marzipan Fantasy Fruits, 51
Painted Foil Sculpture, 42
Paper Bag Sculpture, 46
Royal Icing Art, 50
Salt Ceramic, 39
Stained Glass Cookies, 48
Stomped Foil Sculpture, 41
String Thing, 45
Tissue Mâché, 43
Tissue Mobile, 44

Age 5 & up
Candy Bugs, 53
Paste Batik, 58
Salt Figures, 57
Scrimshaw Pendant, 56
Soap Sculpture, 54
Wire Sculpting, 55

Alphabetical Index of Activities

Materials Index

50 great ways to explore and create using baking soda, shoe polish, vegetable dyes, and other surprising materials!

Painting
MaryAnn F. Kohl

Encourage children to experience the joy of exploration and discovery with this new series by award-winning author MaryAnn F. Kohl. Excerpted from the national best-seller **Preschool Art,** each book in the series emphasizes the process of art, not the product. **Preschool Art: Painting** brings you 50 great ways to paint using vegetable dyes, baking soda, cornstarch, shoe polish, and other surprising materials. Make art fun and accessible to children of all ages with these creative, easy-to-do activities!

ISBN 0-87659-224-8 / Gryphon House / 13596 / $7.95

50 great ways to explore and create with chalk, crayons, stencils, textures, and more!

Drawing
MaryAnn F. Kohl

Encourage children to experience the joy of exploration and discovery with this new series by award-winning author MaryAnn F. Kohl. Excerpted from the national best-seller **Preschool Art,** each book in this new series emphasizes the process of art, not the product. **Preschool Art: Drawing** gives you 50 great ways to create with chalk, crayons, stencils, textures, and more! Make art fun and accessible for children of all ages with these creative, easy-to-do activities.

ISBN 0-87659-223-X / Gryphon House / 19658 / $7.95

Available at your favorite bookstore, school supply store, or order from Gyphon House at 800.638.0928 or www.gryphonhouse.com.

50 great ways to explore and create with lace, string, fabric, glue and other easy-to-find materials!

Craft and Construction

MaryAnn F. Kohl

Encourage children to experience the joy of exploration and discovery with this new series by award-winning author MaryAnn F. Kohl. Excerpted from the national best-seller **Preschool Art,** each book in the series emphasizes the process of art, not the product. **Preschool Art: Craft & Construction** gives you 50 great ways to create with lace, string, fabric, glue, and other simple materials. Make art fun and accessible to children of all ages with these creative, easy-to-do activities!

ISBN 0-87659-251-5 / Gryphon House / 19425 / $7.95

50 great ways to explore and create with paper, feathers, buttons, and other easy-to-find materials!

Collage and Paper

MaryAnn F. Kohl

Encourage children to experience the joy of exploration and discovery with this new series by MaryAnn F. Kohl. Excerpted from the national best-sellers **Preschool Art** and **MathArts,** this book emphasizes the process of art, not the product. **Preschool Art: Collage and Paper** gives you 50 great ways to create with paper, feathers, buttons, and other easy-to-find materials. Make art fun and accessible to children of all ages with these creative, easy-to-do activities!

ISBN 0-87659-252-3 / Gryphon House / 15726 / $7.95

Available at your favorite bookstore, school supply store, or order from Gyphon House at 800.638.0928 or www.gryphonhouse.com.